Dover Castle
A Frontline Fortress and its Wartime Tunnels

Jonathan Coad

VICE ADMIRAL DOVER.

FIXED DEFENCES DOVER

Introduction

Dover Castle's location, overlooking the shortest sea crossing between Britain and mainland Europe, has given it immense strategic importance and ensured its long use as a powerful fortress. Soldiers were stationed here in 1066 by William the Conqueror and the castle almost certainly remained continuously garrisoned until 1958. No other castle in the British Isles can match this length of active military service.

Within the famous white cliffs, hidden from view beneath the castle and safe from bombardment, lies a network of tunnels. They were first excavated in the chalk over 200 years ago. At this time, Britain faced the threat of French invasion, and the government poured money into fortifying the town and port of Dover as well as the castle. The tunnels were dug to provide much needed barracks for some of the thousands of troops quartered here.

By the end of the 19th century the tunnels had been abandoned, but they were brought back into service in the Second World War, when they made their most notable contribution to British history. From 1939 they housed the command centre that controlled naval operations in the Channel, and it was from here that in May 1940 the extraordinary evacuation of the British Army from Dunkirk was planned and coordinated. In the operation, which involved no fewer than 693 British ships, over 338,000 men were rescued. Over the next few years the tunnels were greatly extended to serve both as space for a hospital and as a large combined headquarters, responsible for guarding the Straits of Dover and involved in preparing for the 1944 invasion of Europe.

During the Cold War this network of tunnels was transformed into the secret location of one of Britain's Regional Seats of Government, with the optimistic role of organizing what would be left of life in the event of nuclear attack, among the radioactive carnage of a post-nuclear south-east England.

Above: Vice-Admiral Bertram Ramsay, who masterminded the Dunkirk evacuation in 1940, at his headquarters in the tunnels at Dover Castle

Facing page: Winston Churchill, with the mayor of Dover, emerging from the main wartime entrance to the cliff tunnels during one of his visits to the castle in the Second World War

A Frontline Fortress and the Early Tunnels

From the 1740s onwards, after a long period of neglect, spectacular additions were made to the defences of Dover Castle. At the same time the defences of the town and harbour were greatly strengthened in the face of the threat of invasion from France.

The danger was never greater than during the Napoleonic Wars, and from 1797 onwards an extraordinary complex of tunnels – best known for the role it played during the Second World War – was excavated behind the cliff face to provide underground barracks for some of the thousands of troops stationed at Dover. There was a precedent for tunnel building here: tunnels were first dug beneath the castle almost 800 years ago during the celebrated siege by the French in 1216, and afterwards, underground passages were excavated to reinforce the vulnerable northern defences of the castle.

THE MEDIEVAL TUNNELS

As early as the 1170s and 1180s, when Henry II's castle was being built, the king's engineers had found that chalk was an ideal material from which to cut the castle's great defensive ditches. But it was the great siege of 1216–17 that prompted the building of military tunnels. Prince Louis of France had landed at Thanet in May 1216 in support of the barons who were rebelling against King John, and laid siege to Dover Castle in the autumn. The French forces attacked the northern end of the castle, where Louis' miners tunnelled under the outer defences and caused one of the north gateway towers to collapse. Only a heroic defence by Hubert de Burgh, justiciar of England, and his garrison, saved the castle.

After the siege Hubert greatly strengthened the castle, constructing Constable's and Fitzwilliam gates and blocking the north gate, now known as the Norfolk Towers. In the moat outside he built St John's Tower, and beyond that a massive outwork, or spur, to help to command the high ground to the north. To allow the garrison to reach these defences largely unseen, he excavated a tunnel through the chalk from behind the Norfolk Towers to St John's Tower, cutting through the earlier siege tunnels. A drawbridge linked this to a further short tunnel within the outwork.

The medieval tunnels were enlarged and extended during the Napoleonic Wars when the outwork was strengthened. A caponier, or protected passage, was built on the site of the drawbridge, its gun loops covering the moats on both sides. Two further caponiers fired down the moats and one led to a vaulted guardhouse with remotely controlled doors to the outside, which allowed the guards to control entry. These extraordinary tunnels and later works — completely separate from the tunnels behind the cliff face — can still be visited.

Above: A reconstruction drawing showing Prince Louis' forces tunnelling under the north gate tower during the 1216 siege, which caused it to collapse. It was the French siege that prompted the building of the castle's medieval tunnels

Below: The upper level of the caponier linking St John's Tower with the spur defences. This work dates from the Napoleonic Wars

Facing page: Dover Castle from the Sea (detail), engraved in 1851 by J T Willmore after a painting of 1822 by J M W Turner. The entrance to the Napoleonic tunnels is visible in the cliff face below the castle

Right: The first duke of Dorset returning to the castle in a procession after taking the oath of office as lord warden of the Cinque Ports in 1727. This painting by John Wootton clearly shows the harbour, then located west of the town, in the distance

Below: Reconstruction of a scene inside one of the mid-18th-century barracks at Dover Castle. These barracks in the inner bailey are some of the oldest in the country

A REDUNDANT FORTRESS

The later tunnels behind the cliff face were built for a completely different military reason from their medieval counterparts. Well before 1700 Dover Castle was largely obsolete as a fortress. The scale of its surviving medieval defences, mostly erected between 1160 and 1260, with their concentric lines of curtain walls and towers and heavily fortified gateways, remained a vivid symbol of royal power. But the introduction of effective artillery in the latter part of the 15th century hastened the decline of castles whose tall walls and towers offered little protection against such weapons. New designs of artillery fortresses had to be developed, and from

the 1530s Henry VIII's military engineers built a series of artillery forts along the south coast, such as those at Deal and Walmer castles, to guard likely landing places. At Dover Castle – almost as a token – a few guns were placed near the cliff-top and in the 16th century a small battery was sited in the western moat.

Although it was mostly disused, the castle provided a convenient lodging for officials travelling between England and the Continent, with accommodation for the small garrison, generally a master gunner and a few gunners. The official residence of the lord warden of the Cinque Ports remained in Constable's Gate until 1708, when it was transferred to Walmer. But in the early 1690s the castle was being described as 'ruinous', its military role seemingly long over.

THE CASTLE REVIVED

Paradoxically, the weapon responsible for Dover Castle's decline was about to lead to its renaissance. By the 16th century field armies were increasingly being equipped with heavy guns. For an invading army coming by sea it was no longer possible to disembark, as William the Conqueror had done, on a convenient beach, and live off the land. A port had to be captured so that the cumbersome guns and other supplies could be safely unloaded. In the 1740s, with Britain at war with Spain and France and threatened by a Jacobite

invasion, the government realized the vulnerability of Dover and its port. From then onwards, Dover's defences were to be strengthened in every European war involving Britain. Military planners feared that invading forces might land on the coast near Folkestone or Walmer, march swiftly overland and capture Dover from the rear. Gradually, town and port were protected by encircling fortifications.

Within the castle itself, the most urgent requirement was for additional accommodation for a larger garrison. Between 1745 and 1756 a series of barracks was constructed in the inner bailey, and the great tower was adapted to house a further 226 soldiers. The barracks, built by the military engineer John Desmaretz, still survive. Desmaretz also remodelled the northern defences from Avranches Tower to the Norfolk Towers for heavy artillery and built Bell Battery and Four Gun Battery, commanding the road from Walmer. These works marked the first major additions to the castle's defences for 500 years. In the early 1780s, during the War of American Independence, the existing harbour defences of Moat's Bulwark and Archcliffe Fort were strengthened by Guilford, North, Townsend and Amherst batteries (see page 8), built between them along the foreshore.

The threat of invasion was never greater than during the Revolutionary and Napoleonic Wars (1793–1815), when there were even more spectacular additions to the castle's defences. The military engineer Lieutenant-Colonel William Twiss (see page 10) continued Desmaretz's work, employing hundreds of workmen and soldiers. He reformed the ramparts for artillery and deepened and widened the rest of the outer moat. Outside this, Horseshoe, Hudson's, East Arrow, East Demi- and Constable's bastions were constructed to provide flanking fire, and the spur at the castle's northern tip was remodelled, incorporating and expanding the medieval tunnels. To allow artillery to command the high ground north of the castle, he replaced the roof of Henry II's great tower with massive brick vaults to support guns on top; and he built Canon's Gate to aid troop movements between castle and town. Across the town he fortified Western Heights with the largest and most astonishing defence works built in Britain during the Napoleonic wars. Together, these works ensured that Dover had its most vulnerable approaches well protected.

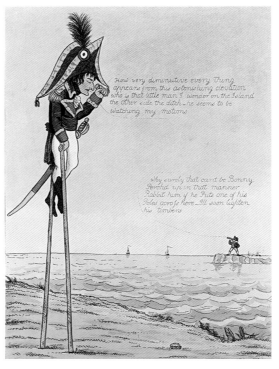

Above: Bell Battery, added to the castle in 1756, was part of the work carried out at Dover Castle by the military engineer John Desmaretz

Left: Cartoon of about 1800, showing Napoleon Bonaparte looking over the Dover Straits at John Bull, symbolizing England, on the white cliffs

Above: A view of Dover Castle from the new fortifications under construction on Western Heights, from an 1808 painting by Captain John Durrant. The sentry stands beside a bell tent, which was probably being used as a guard post pending completion of the fortifications

Right: The late 18th- and 19th-century defences of the town and harbour at Dover, superimposed on a modern map of the town and docks

THE NAPOLEONIC TUNNELS

Quartering the huge numbers of troops needed to man these new defences, and to provide a mobile force to fight an invading army on the beachheads, presented major problems. Many soldiers were accommodated in the town, and hutted and tented camps were established on Western Heights while the fortifications there were being completed. In

the castle itself the problem was acute, with every available space in use for storage or accommodation. The existing barracks in the inner bailey were far from adequate, although they were supplemented by temporary timber ones south of Palace Gate and later by new casemates at Canon's Gate and to the rear of the Norfolk Towers.

In 1797 a radical solution was adopted to house the troops. Although documentary evidence is sketchy, the idea was almost certainly the brainchild of William Twiss. Because of the lack of space for further barracks above ground in the castle, a decision was taken to excavate tunnels in from the cliff face to use as underground accommodation. As medieval engineers had already found, the chalk cliff on which the castle stands was comparatively easy to excavate and generally stable. The Georgian military engineers also had recent first-hand practical experience of tunnel building. During the famous siege of Gibraltar (1779–83) they had built extensive tunnels for gun positions high on the Rock to

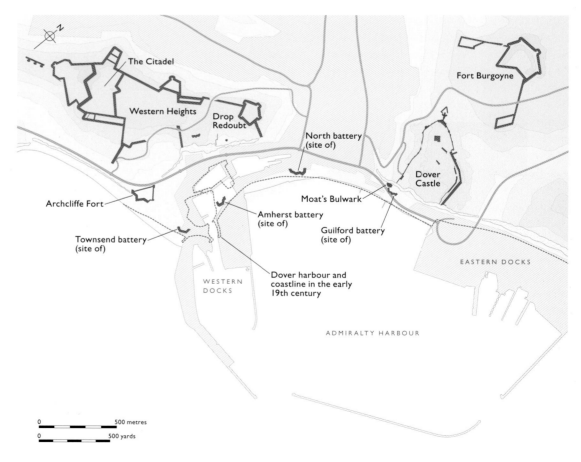

0 _____ 500 metres

0 _____ 500 yards

bombard the Spanish lines. Nearer home at Chatham, a series of tunnels provided access to gun positions in the Barrier Ditch below Fort Amherst. At Dover Castle engineers had just completed a 400 ft (120m) deep well just south of Palace Gate to provide good supplies of drinking water for the enlarged garrison, and Horseshoe and Hudson's bastions were being linked to the interior of the castle by elaborate communication tunnels. A little later the engineers were to install a remarkable network of small, oval, brick-lined sewers. These replaced a large number of insanitary cesspits and linked the barrack latrines with a central drain tunnelled to the foot of the cliff, where it discharged into the sea.

At that date, no similar underground barracks existed in Britain, but their use at Dover had many advantages apart from saving space. They would be totally impervious to any form of artillery barrage if the castle were besieged, while their front entrances were too high up the cliffs to be threatened by bombardment from enemy warships. Their main entrances could be approached easily down a sloping ramp from the southern side of the castle.

In 1797 four tunnels, or 'subterraneous bombproofs' as they were known, were driven in from the cliff face to form soldiers' accommodation. The evidence suggests that the soldiers' tunnels then, as now, had two floors: the upper floors were of timber and were approached by staircases midway along the two outer tunnels. In 1798 three further, and larger, tunnels were excavated a little way to the east of this group for the use of officers who, following the custom of the Georgian army, were given much more spacious accommodation, probably all on one level. The seven tunnels were linked near the cliff face by a winding communications tunnel which also gave access to the well and the latrines. Another passage or 'gallery of communication' ran to the

William Twiss (1745–1827)

As well as his work at Dover Castle, Twiss vastly extended the fortifications of Western Heights on the other side of the town

Modernizing Dover's defences in the Napoleonic Wars was the climax of William Twiss's distinguished career as a Royal Engineer. As a young man he had trained for two years in the Tower of London Drawing Office, and then served in the dockyard towns of Portsmouth, Plymouth and Gibraltar, gaining experience of naval works, before being posted to America in 1776 during the War of Independence. There he organized the movement of some 500 boats to Lake Champlain, which allowed the British to take control of the lake from the Americans, and planned the siege works that led to the taking of Fort Ticonderoga. Captured at the battle of Saratoga in 1777, he was exchanged for American prisoners and sent to Canada, where he spent the next six years strengthening the country's defences, eventually becoming chief engineer. In 1779 he built the Coteau-du-Lac Canal, the first with locks in North America, an experience that proved useful later during construction of the Royal Military Canal on Romney Marsh.

Twiss returned to England in 1783 and in 1792 was appointed commanding Royal Engineer for the southern military district. Fears of invasion prompted a huge increase in defence works and Twiss remained in this post until he retired in 1809. As well as his work at Dover Castle, he vastly extended the fortifications of Western Heights on the other side of the town. He had a major role in the design and location of the 74 martello towers along the Kent and Sussex coasts and also rebuilt Fort Cumberland at Portsmouth. After his retirement he moved to Bingley, in Yorkshire, where he lived comfortably, employed eight gardeners, and was carried around the town in a sedan chair by liveried servants.

rear of the tunnels, linking them to a second entrance within the castle just above Canon's Gate. The seaward ends of the tunnels had brick fronts with doors and windows, their design similar to contemporary casemate fronts.

The work would have been supervised by the military engineers under Twiss, but the actual excavation work, using hand tools, was largely done by troops from the various militias then at Dover, a number of which came from mining areas. As the miners burrowed out this extraordinary complex, the weather-beaten warships of Admiral Duncan's North Sea forces patrolling the Straits of Dover would have been frequently visible from their cliff vantage point. In the autumn of 1797, Duncan's hard-fought victory over the Dutch at Camperdown had put fresh heart into the Royal Navy's resolve to keep the revolutionary fervour of France firmly on the far side of the Channel.

Although the soft chalk had aided the military engineers and enabled them to complete their tunnelling by the end of 1798, it posed some problems of stability. In February 1799 there was a serious fall of chalk near the well, as Thomas Pattenden, a draper and stocking seller who lived in Dover, recorded in his diary on 16 February:

'This week there was a very great fall of the cliff exact between the soldiers and the officers subterraneous barracks, where the opening is between to give light to the Well. It fell down quite from the top of the Cliff a very great way. This day in the forenoon it was discovered that unknown to any person in the night, a bank of chalk and earth had fell down by the frost and thaw and filled one of the huts in the Castle, whereby an Artillery man and his wife were suffocated as they lay in bed, the infant child was preserved and taken out alive.'

Probably for reasons of safety as much as for health, the accommodation tunnels were largely brick-lined, although this work was not apparently completed before the end of 1810. Their distinguished parabolic profiles match those of contemporary casemates on Western Heights.

Below: A view of the cliffs and beach below the castle, painted by Captain Durrant in 1809. The painting clearly shows the openings in the cliff face for the soldiers' tunnels, built on two levels, to the left, and the three officers' tunnels on the right. At the foot of the cliffs is part of Guilford Battery

LIFE IN THE TUNNELS

Pressure on accommodation was such that the first troops were moved in here certainly by the summer of 1798, with construction work presumably continuing around them. No contemporary accounts have been discovered of life in these strange underground barracks during the Napoleonic Wars. A description of the castle in 1812 refers to 'several underground barracks, particularly the Royal Billy … where one room will contain 500 men', suggesting that perhaps on occasion as many as 2,000 troops could have been quartered here.

There were surprisingly few practical problems associated with such underground accommodation. Through-ventilation was provided by vertical shafts at the rear of the tunnels connecting to the surface overhead; fireplaces in the accommodation tunnel walls had their flues similarly linked, and a central well was sunk for fresh water. Sanitation was provided by a group of latrines between the tunnels that discharged

Above: A painting of about 1840 by William Burgess showing soldiers on the terrace marching down to the cliff barracks

Right: A similar view of the cliff balcony today

through drains to the sea. Except for those soldiers who were quartered at the front of the tunnels, lack of daylight was perhaps the most serious disadvantage. This would have been mitigated to an extent by lime-washing the walls and vaults and by the use of lanterns and candles. In practice, the level of illumination was probably no worse than that experienced by sailors on the middle or lower gun decks of one of the Royal Navy's contemporary line-of-battleships with its gun-ports closed.

Apart from the novelty of living underground, soldiers arriving here for the first time must have been astounded by the size of these spaces. Nearly all contemporary barracks had rooms designed to house between 8 and 30 men, and the barracks then being built by Twiss on Western Heights had narrow rooms, each for 14 men. Within these, the soldiers lived, slept and ate with their room-mates. There were no central cookhouses or messes – the men prepared their rations in their rooms and cooked them on the barrack-room fires.

How this worked in practice in such huge underground barracks is a matter for speculation. Dimly lit and probably noisy, with limited warmth, a perpetual smell of stale food mixed with that of unwashed bodies, and condensation probably dripping from the roofs when the barracks were full, the tunnels must have been uncomfortable to live in, if secure. Perhaps significantly, we know that the troops here were among the first to be provided with iron bedsteads, considered to be more hygienic than wooden ones, which harboured vermin such as fleas and lice.

Later subdivision of most of the barrack tunnels in the 20th century has obscured something of their scale, but the great brick vaults remain as completed. Some of the fireplaces that once provided heat and cooking facilities survive, although most have subsequently been blocked. Admiralty Casemate, the easternmost of the three officers' tunnels, is the only one to retain a timber floor that pre-dates its reuse in the Second World War. Here the marks of the office partitions installed for the Navy are visible on the brick walls, and the wartime ducts for the forced-air ventilation marks the narrow passage which linked these offices. In parts of the unlined communication tunnels it is still possible to see

pick marks made by the Georgian miners in the chalk. The small chamber with a brick domed roof, beside the communication tunnel that links the original three eastern tunnels to the cliff terrace, marks the top of the solitary well shaft: this was cut deep into the underlying chalk to provide water for the soldiers quartered here.

Left: A recruiting party from an infantry regiment in a village street, about 1770. Although most soldiers enlisted willingly, many 'took the king's shilling' in ignorance, tricked when plied with drink or lured by the promises of recruiting parties
Below left: The unlined communications tunnel linking the seven main tunnels
Below: Graffiti on the tunnel walls, covering the period from 1860 to 1942

Above: A party of fishermen, smugglers, or perhaps both, on Dover beach, depicted in an early 19th-century engraving
Below: *Soldiers firing Congreve rockets, like those stored in the cliff tunnels, from earthworks in 1827 (right); Congreve rockets from the 1820s (left)*

THE COAST BLOCKADE

Victory at Waterloo in 1815 led to the rapid reduction of the British Army to its peacetime strength. Barracks above ground within the castle, together with new accommodation for 1,500 men on Western Heights, were more than adequate for the troops then at Dover, and the cliff tunnels ceased to be used as military quarters.

The tunnels were given a variety of new uses, however. For some time the three eastern tunnels became huge gunpowder magazines and stores for Congreve rockets. The latter were first fired a few weeks after the battle of Trafalgar in 1805, during an unsuccessful attack on Boulogne by Sir Sidney Smith, one of Nelson's commanders.

Some of the remaining tunnels were used in the long-running war against smugglers, hitherto waged largely at sea by cutters of the Revenue Service. The high rates of duty imposed on wine, spirits and other goods coming in from the Continent at this time made smuggling a lucrative venture for fishermen and seafarers, and in some parts of the country it was more economically significant than legal occupations such as farming and fishing. With the ending of the wars with France, efforts to eradicate smuggling were redoubled. In 1817 the Admiralty accepted proposals by Captain Joseph McCulloch to set up a 'Coast Blockade' along the Kent coast. McCulloch's scheme involved basing naval seamen in the charge of lieutenants at a number of 'blockade stations' and mounting foot patrols along the beaches. Some of the bloodiest battles between smugglers and the authorities were to result.

At Dover in 1818 two officers and 22 men of the blockade service made their base in two of the western tunnels. These were isolated from the castle above, and linked to the beach below by a zigzag ramp cut down the face of the cliff by the Royal Engineers. The blockade service was stationed here for more than eight years. In July 1826 a skirmish with smugglers on the beach below led to the murder of Quartermaster Richard Morgan of the blockade, killed by the

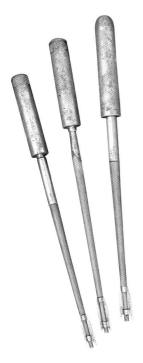

Left: This etching by William Heath of the East Cliff, dated 1836, shows the cliff entrance to the tunnels. This is presumably where the Coast Blockade had access to the beach below

Below left: This cartoon by Thomas Rowlandson from about 1810 shows a woman smuggler being 'rigged out' with brandy, perfume, cigars, teas and other contraband, which she will hide beneath her dress

smugglers' guns. Nobody claimed the very substantial reward of £500 for information leading to the murderers, but from other evidence it was apparent that this was the work of the last of the Kent gangs, the Aldington gang (known as the Blues). Ten weeks later, blockade officers and Bow Street Runners raided the village of Aldington at 3am and caught the gang leaders in their beds.

With the break-up of this gang, large-scale smuggling in Kent was virtually at an end. By this time, the Coast Blockade officers were finding their cliff accommodation inconveniently far from the beach in an emergency, and by 1828 they had obtained permission to relocate to the Congreve Rocket Shed beside Guilford Battery below the castle. The rockets were removed to the cliff tunnels and stored there alongside the gunpowder barrels that occupied much of the space.

In 1856, together with new barracks for the troops, work began on the vast surviving Officers' New Barracks, designed by Anthony Salvin to house 45 officers and a mess. In the same year the tunnels were again used briefly as barracks by the British Swiss Legion, mercenaries recruited from 1855 for service in the Crimean War. It was probably at this time too that communications with the tunnels were improved by a stone double spiral staircase, cut from the surface nearby to provide a link to the rear communications passage.

For a number of years ammunition continued to be stored in part of the complex before

being removed, perhaps as late as the 1870s following the construction of Hospital and Shot Yard batteries on the cliff edge above. These were armed with new shell-firing guns that required different storage arrangements for their ammunition. Certainly before the end of the 19th century the tunnels seem to have been abandoned, although they may well have been used in part for occasional storage by the garrison.

DOVER IN THE FIRST WORLD WAR

By 1851 the castle was described as 'unarmed', although some bastions retained increasingly obsolete weapons. As late as 1853 the walls and gateways of the inner bailey were remodelled by military engineers to improve their defensive capabilities, and a caponier was constructed across the eastern moat at Ashford Lower Flank as a covered access to Hudson's Bastion. These were the last significant alterations to the castle: completion of Fort Burgoyne in 1865 immediately to the north effectively ended its role as a 'First Class Fortress'. Nonetheless, the castle remained the garrison headquarters for the powerful ring of defences evolving round the town and for the huge Admiralty Harbour, which was completed early in the 20th century. The harbour's size reflected its roles as a commercial port, a harbour of refuge for ships needing shelter and a wartime naval base.

By 1905 advances in ordnance technology enabled coastal artillery around the harbour to be controlled from a central Fire Command Post built on the cliff edge over the 1870s Hospital Battery, the guns of which had become obsolete by 1890. The commanding position of the Fire Command Post, overlooking the harbour and Dover Straits, led the Admiralty in 1914 to site its Port War Signal Station on top of it. From here the Navy controlled the movements of all ships into and out of the harbour using flags and wireless and could quickly liaise with the gunners immediately below.

These two installations, now known as Admiralty Look-out, played notable roles in both world wars.

During the First World War naval headquarters in Dover occupied three terraced houses on Marine Parade, close to the harbour. From here Flag Officer Dover directed naval operations. Warships of the Dover Patrol were responsible for the safe passage of troop and supply convoys to France, guarding the Straits against German submarines and warships, and maintaining the huge minefields and anti-submarine nets that eventually stretched across to the French shore.

The wartime garrison in the town increased to some 16,000 troops. These manned coastal guns and guarded the area against potential raids or possible invasion; garrison headquarters remained at the castle. On 21 December 1914 the first recorded bombing raid by a German plane on Britain took place at Dover when a bomb was dropped off the harbour. One consequence was that Dover became one of the earliest towns to be provided with anti-aircraft guns and searchlights. One of the searchlights was placed on a turret on the great tower, itself in use as an armoury and ammunition store. A military hospital occupied parts of Constable's Gate. The use of the tunnels during the war remains largely unknown, but they may well have been used to store equipment for garrison troops and engineers. Reserve rations for 5,500 men for seven days were also kept somewhere in the castle in case troops were forced to retreat to it.

Right: A rare photograph of the eastern defences of the castle during the First World War, showing the army camp established in the valley below (Hudson's Bastion is to the left and Horseshoe Bastion in the centre)

Left: The Fire Command Post, from where a watch was kept for enemy warships and unidentified ships. Information from here and other observation posts was fed to the Fire Commander in the adjacent chart room

Below: The entrance to Dover harbour in 1918, by Sir John Lavery. The fleet can be seen in the harbour, and a seaplane is landing in the centre; in the foreground are the nets to prevent enemy submarines from entering the harbour

The Tunnels in the Second World War

In the Second World War Dover Castle stood in the front line, directly facing German-occupied France, a mere 22 miles across the narrow Straits of Dover. The Napoleonic tunnels were brought back into use, and for nine days in late May and early June 1940 they became the nerve centre controlling Operation Dynamo – the rescue of allied forces from Dunkirk, one of the greatest and most successful evacuations in history.

For the rest of the war, the tunnels continued to play a vital role in the war effort, ultimately being used from 1943 as a combined headquarters for all three services. Later, during the Cold War, the tunnels were secretly equipped and modernized to serve as a Regional Seat of Government in the event of a nuclear attack, and remained on the secret list until they were abandoned in 1984.

1938: PREPARATIONS FOR WAR

After the First World War, coastal gun batteries were placed on a 'care and maintenance' basis and the castle resumed its peacetime role as a garrison headquarters. It was home to the Royal Garrison Artillery, which was responsible for the coastal guns, until 1924, after which the territorial section of the Kent and Sussex Regiment of Royal Artillery took on the maintenance of these guns. The castle reverted to being an infantry headquarters, initially for the 1st Battalion, the King's Own Yorkshire Light Infantry.

The same year, reflecting the needs of the new garrison, Long Gun Magazine and its surrounding earth blast banks west of the Officers' New Barracks were buried and the site levelled to provide an additional parade ground. Outside the castle on the eastern side three new barrack blocks were constructed with improved facilities for the soldiers, largely replacing the now obsolete 18th-century barracks in the inner bailey. The tunnels seem to have remained mostly deserted, although for part of the time three of the four western ones were allocated as stores for the Royal Engineers. The growing threat in the late 1930s of war with Germany, however, was to result in a new and very different role for both the castle and its tunnels.

The Czech crisis of 1938 saw the British fleet mobilized in September, the Dover coastal guns manned in October and British Prime Minister Neville Chamberlain flying to Munich to secure a peace agreement with Hitler. In September Rear-Admiral Bertram Ramsay was recalled from retirement and given the task of re-establishing a headquarters for the Flag Officer Dover. This was to prove an inspired choice (see feature, page 20).

By this time, the Spanish Civil War had demonstrated all too clearly the destructive power of heavy bombers. A secure naval headquarters at Dover was now essential and the old Napoleonic tunnels provided the ideal solution. They overlooked the harbour, were impervious to bombing and lay conveniently close to the Port War Signal Station. By early 1939, planning was well under way to equip the tunnels as the hub of defence operations at Dover. The easternmost tunnel was selected by Ramsay, and became Admiralty Casemate. The next two tunnels were to house the coastal artillery operations room,

with a separate gun operations room for the anti-aircraft defences. The fortress commander's staff joined them at the end of May 1940. Lighting and ventilation were improved and telephone and radio communications installed. The main tunnels were partitioned to create a multitude of offices, meeting rooms and operation rooms. Except in emergencies, staff would not sleep here. Deep in the cliffs behind the naval base huge caverns were cut for secure storage for 45,000 tons of furnace oil and 5,000 tons of diesel oil for the Navy's warships.

Above: Vice-Admiral Ramsay's cabin at the end of Admiralty Casemate, photographed in the early years of the war. From here he had a view over the harbour to the Channel beyond. The tape on the window was to minimize splinters from shell or bomb blasts

Below: A reconstruction of the guard room in Casemate level of the tunnels

Facing page: Prime Minister Winston Churchill on the Casemate balcony on 28 August 1940, watching an air battle during the Battle of Britain

Right: Winston Churchill studies reports of the action that day with Vice-Admiral Bertram Ramsay in the Casemate tunnels on 28 August 1940

Below right: Ramsay on the Casemate balcony in April 1941

Sir Bertram Home Ramsay

'Admiral Ramsay's courage, drive and skill as an organizer enabled us to retrieve sufficient from the wreck to begin to build again'

Ramsay, who had joined the Royal Navy as a cadet in 1898, first showed his talent for organization early in his career, when he collaborated with the Army during the Somaliland expedition in 1903, and quickly earned a reputation as an outstanding organizer. He served during the First World War in the famous Dover Patrol, latterly in command of HMS *Broke*, and so knew the area well. Recalled from early retirement in 1938 to re-activate the Dover command, he played a pivotal role in organizing the Dunkirk evacuation, and went on to have an important part in the allied landings in North Africa and Sicily.

Four years after Operation Dynamo, as allied naval commander-in-chief for the Normandy invasion, Ramsay masterminded Operation Neptune, the naval side of the D-Day landings, and was responsible for the biggest and most successful invasion fleet in history. He was killed in an air crash in France on 2 January 1945, and was buried at Saint Germain-en-Laye, near his headquarters, with full naval honours.

In a moving tribute, the First Lord of the Admiralty recorded that 'Admiral Ramsay's courage, drive and skill as an organizer enabled us [at Dunkirk] to retrieve sufficient from the wreck to begin to build again, and to carry on in faith at a time when the world believed that we were defeated.'

THE OUTBREAK OF WAR

Ten days before war broke out in September 1939 Ramsay, shortly to be appointed as Vice-Admiral Dover, returned to the castle. Much still remained to be done. In a letter to his wife in late August he wrote:

> 'Here we are struggling with the difficult problem of trying to set up a naval base and at the same time to operate it as though it was already established. We have no stationery, books, typists or machines, no chairs and few tables, maddening communications. I pray … that war, if it has to come, will be averted for yet a few days.'

He also found only five 3-inch anti-aircraft guns protecting the harbour.

All was to change rapidly, as his organizational skills and his ability to inspire his staff were shown. On the outbreak of war, two vast minefields were meticulously laid in the Straits and patrolled by armed trawlers to prevent the passage of German submarines. By the end of October 1939 four had been destroyed, forcing the German navy to send U-boats round Scotland, which restricted their Atlantic patrol times. Meanwhile, the British Expeditionary Force (BEF) and its supplies were safely transported to France; sea routes were swept for German mines and made safe for merchant ships. Vessels in the harbour lay behind submarine booms and were further protected by coastal gun batteries, barrage balloons and an increasing ring of anti-aircraft guns, all controlled from the underground headquarters at the castle.

The winter of 1939–40 was exceptionally cold, with heavy snowfalls. In mid-March 1940, on one of his three visits to Dover over that period, King George VI was conducted by Ramsay in a blizzard on a tour of inspection to the eastern breakwater and naval base, before being revived by hot tea and whisky and taken to see the underground headquarters. There, not all went according to plan. As Ramsay later told his wife, the king:

> 'enjoyed himself in the mine galleries and in the casemates, but would you believe it? The current failed just as we arrived and out went the lights and the heaters. Really it was rotten luck as he did want to warm his hands.'

Such royal visits boosted the morale of the garrison and the Navy, while at that stage of the conflict there was little to suggest that Dover's role would be any different from the one it had played during the First World War.

Below: King George VI, in naval uniform, at Dover in March 1940, watching British reinforcements embarking for France

Right: Troops of the British Expeditionary Force marching through the ruined port of Dunkirk in May 1940. The retreat was desperate, with heavy fighting. The BEF destroyed or disabled most of its tanks, artillery and transport, since they could not be embarked and would be useful to the enemy

Below: The rapid German advance between 10 and 30 May 1940. Within a few weeks they had broken through to the French coast, effectively cutting off the British and some French troops from the main French army and trapping them within an ever-diminishing pocket around the port of Dunkirk

DOVER AND THE DUNKIRK EVACUATION

On 10 May 1940 the 'phoney war' abruptly ended as Hitler's armies struck westwards, through neutral Belgium and Holland, bypassing the Maginot Line and French armies on the Franco-German frontier. As the BEF and French forces advanced into Holland and Belgium that morning to counter the Germans, Ramsay despatched eight destroyers from Dover, four to protect the left flank of the French 7th army from air attack as it advanced along the Belgian coast. The other four carried demolition parties to blow up Dutch and Belgian harbour installations, oil tanks and anything usable by the enemy. Before Holland surrendered on 15 May, several hundred self-propelled barges, or schuytes, and 50 tugs had left Antwerp and other ports for England.

The German Advance (14 May)

On 14 May the Germans broke through the French army at Sedan on the river Meuse, which allowed them to advance towards the coast largely unimpeded. Within five days Panzer (tank) forces had captured Amiens and reached the coast at Abbeville, leaving the BEF, the French 7th and part of the 1st armies, and the Belgian army severed from main French forces to the south and forced to retreat to a diminishing pocket of land around the port of Dunkirk.

The speed and ferocity of the German advance continued unabated. On 22 May Boulogne was cut off, as was Calais soon afterwards. In a foretaste of events to come, Ramsay sent over demolition parties and troops to both ports to aid rearguards holding the perimeters, while destroyers and channel steamers evacuated the wounded and other troops. The destroyers sustained heavy casualties, their guns engaging German forces around the towns and as they advanced along the quays. In a scribbled note to his wife, Ramsay wrote:

'Poor Captain D. (Simson) was killed on the bridge of the *Keith* by a machine gun bullet, and I have lost the captains of two other destroyers. I get new destroyers daily and throw them into the fray where they remain until they are so damaged they have to be sent away.'

In all, these missions rescued some 5,500 men.

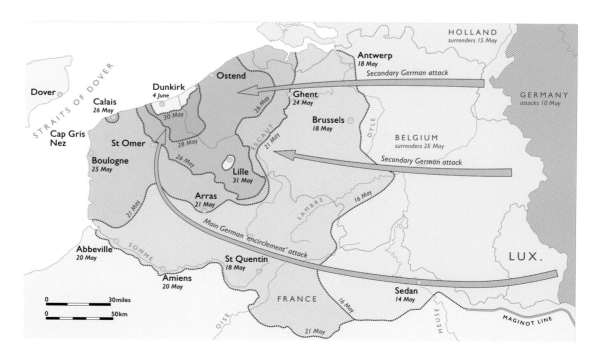

Left: *A German Panzer regiment crossing the river Meuse at Sedan, France, on 14 May 1940. From here the German forces made a rapid advance towards the coast*

Boulogne fell on 25 May, followed the next day by Calais. That evening the British government ordered the evacuation of as many men as possible of the 400,000 BEF and allied troops trapped within a diminishing perimeter centred on Dunkirk. The new prime minister, Winston Churchill, warned the country to prepare for 'hard and heavy tidings'.

Preparations for Operation Dynamo (20–25 May)

Ramsay had had less than a week to prepare for the operation, code-named Dynamo. By 26 May he had assembled 15 passenger ferries at Dover and a further 20 at Southampton. These, it was hoped, would be able to embark troops directly from the quays at Dunkirk. To help in the evacuation and to provide escorts for the merchant ships Ramsay had a force of destroyers, corvettes, minesweepers and naval trawlers. These ships were augmented by cargo vessels, coasters and some 40 of the Dutch schuytes, known to the Navy who manned them as 'skoots'. All ships of the British merchant marine had their normal civilian crews, both men and women. But as sheer exhaustion and the near-continuous bombing and shelling took their

toll, naval personnel were drafted in to help. As well as these vesssels there were a substantial number of French naval and civilian ships, together with Belgian and Dutch vessels, a Polish destroyer and a Norwegian merchant ship.

Behind this effort lay frantic round-the-clock work in the cliff tunnels. A naval staff officer called it 'organised chaos'. The telephone calls were endless: calls to the Nore Command of the Royal Navy for further destroyers; calls to the Ministry of Shipping for merchant ships; liaison with Southern Railway for special troop trains; and calls to the Admiralty for tugs, weapons, ammunition, medical supplies, spare parts, fuel, rations and above all, trained personnel. On 23 May Ramsay wrote to his wife: 'no bed for any of us last night and probably not for many nights'. Two days later, he wrote again: 'days and nights are all one', and a little later reported that 'All my staff are completely worn out, yet I see no prospect of any let up.' On 27 May some relief was provided by the arrival of Vice-Admiral Sir James Somerville. As the military situation worsened, naval plans repeatedly had to be changed, revised or abandoned. Instant decisions had to be made, frequently from confused and conflicting messages.

Right: Troops on the beach at Dunkirk awaiting evacuation
Below: Captain William Tennant, later Acting Vice-Admiral, in 1944. He worked closely with Ramsay as Senior Naval Officer Ashore at Dunkirk, and went on to play an important role in the Normandy landings in 1944
Below right: The evacuation routes between the Dunkirk beaches and Dover

Operation Dynamo Begins (26–28 May)

At 18.57 on 26 May 1940 Ramsay received the formal signal to commence Operation Dynamo. At best, the Admiralty hoped that 45,000 troops might be saved in the two days before Dunkirk was expected to fall. On 28 May Ramsay told his wife:

'I am directing … one of the most difficult and hazardous operations ever conceived, and unless the good God is very kind, there will be many tragedies attached to it. … For 17 days now I have conducted a series of heart-breaking operations, each with its own tragedies.'

Minefields and shelling from German batteries on the French coast were forcing evacuation convoys to take longer routes to Dunkirk. For some vessels and crews, this was their fourth evacuation task under fire, having already served in operations off the Dutch coast and at Boulogne and Calais. The first convoy, after sustaining heavy air attacks, found Dunkirk port bombed and ablaze. Only the *Royal Daffodil* and the *Canterbury* succeeded in berthing. By the end of the first day only 7,500 troops had been rescued and it was clear that it would be impossible to rely on using the port facilities alone.

At Dunkirk, Captain William Tennant, who was in charge of the naval shore party marshalling the troops for embarkation, diverted rescue ships to the beaches east of the town. But shallow waters meant that even at high tide a destroyer could not approach within a mile of the shore and troops had to be ferried out in ships' lifeboats and small craft. With few small boats available, rescue was painfully slow. The only possible alternative was a spindly concrete mole with a narrow timber walkway running out some 1,300m from the eastern side of the harbour. It was not designed to withstand ships berthing against it, but in this dire emergency it was worth trying.

At 22.30 on the night of 27 May, Tennant ordered the *Queen of the Channel* alongside.

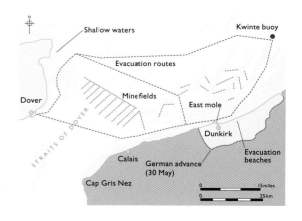

Nine hundred and fifty men scrambled aboard, and though the ship was to be sunk on her way back to Dover, she had proved that the mole was usable. From then on, small ships still operated off the beaches, but large vessels queued for the mole. Differences in loading speeds were dramatic: HMS *Sabre* took two hours to load 100 men from the beach, but alongside the mole 500 troops boarded in 35 minutes.

Beneath Dover Castle, Ramsay was desperate for additional destroyers. More were sent from Portsmouth, and others from the Nore Command. HMS *Jaguar* sped down from convoy duties off Norway, while others came from the Western Approaches of the British Isles. Dover harbour was crowded with vessels unloading, taking on fresh supplies and returning across the Straits. The wounded were helped ashore, and many of the more serious casualties were tended by medical staff on the quaysides; troops in many cases were given their first food for days before boarding special trains. The story was repeated at Folkestone, Ramsgate, Margate, Sheerness and Harwich. On 28 May the Chief of the Air Staff sent a signal to the Royal Air Force:

> 'Today is likely to be the most critical day ever experienced by the British Army. The extreme gravity of the situation should be explained to all units. I am confident that all ranks will

Left: Boarding a destroyer from the eastern mole at Dunkirk. Despite the dangers, embarkation from the mole proved much speedier than from the beaches
Below: Troops wading out shoulder-deep to a rescue ship. The shallow beaches made it impossible for large vessels to get close to the shore

appreciate that it is the duty of the RAF to make their greatest efforts today to assist their comrades of both the army and navy.'

That day the RAF flew over 300 sorties, adding further fighter planes the following day. But the Germans had an advantage in having captured airfields comparatively close to the battleground; the sheer weight of their fighters and bombers was not always easy to deflect and casualties were unavoidable.

A Naval View

Vic Viner, leading seaman with a Royal Navy landing party at Bray-Dunes, remembers:
'I went on the destroyer *Esk*, and they distributed us to the beaches. … When we got near, in shore, the captain said, "Your job … is to take the ship's whaler and the motor boat, and bring these lads off from the beach." … Our first trip we picked up 18 soldiers, complete with all their kit of course, and rowed back and the surf was running. We did four trips.

'… The following morning about 4 o'clock it all became calm … it was much easier to get them into line to wade out onto the little ships, and the little ships took the burden. They were so shattered, but all of them were saying, "We've got to the sea! We'll be saved. We've seen the sea!" And that's all they wanted to do. All we wanted to do was get off the beach, onto the ships and away.'

Right: The Little Ships at Dunkirk in June 1940, *by Norman Wilkinson*

Below right: *Small craft on their way up the Thames in London on 4 June 1940, after taking part in the evacuation*

Below: *A WRNS switchboard operator on duty in the Casemate tunnels, drawn by Robert Sargent Austin*

'We used to go down to the quay and meet the troops coming off the boats … We expected them to be overjoyed to be home, but they walked like automatons, too tired for any emotion. They didn't know then that what looked like defeat would pass into the language as a refusal to be defeated.'
Daphne Baker, née Humphrys, a WRNS officer who worked in the tunnels during the Dunkirk evacuation

The 'Little Ships' (29 May)

In London, the Admiralty's Small Vessels Pool was busy collecting all readily available seaworthy pleasure craft. They came from the Thames, the Medway, east coast ports, and the harbours and creeks of southern England. Volunteer crews, many of whom had never sailed out of sight of land before, were organized into flotillas to sail to Sheerness dockyard. Here, the Navy checked the boats, issued fuel, rations and charts, and sent the boats round in convoys to Ramsgate for final sailing orders.

In all, more than 200 small craft sailed to Dunkirk. Most acted as tenders ferrying troops from the beaches to ships lying offshore, but a significant number of troops returned to England in these vessels, 78 of which were lost during the evacuation.

These pleasure craft were joined by a multitude of other ships: fishing smacks, RNLI lifeboats, trawlers, drifters, the Hayling Island ferries, the Leigh-on-Sea cockle boats. Fifty-six lifeboats, of which 39 were lost, came from liners in port. To tow these and other craft, 40 tugs were sent by the great towage companies –

the London docks had only one tug left, and Newhaven, Portsmouth and Southampton were similarly denuded. The London Fire Brigade fire-float *Massey Shaw* made four trips to the beaches. Perhaps the most unlikely ships to take

part were 25 Thames spritsail barges, with their distinctive brown sails. Nearly a third of these were lost in the operation, but the sailing barges nevertheless rescued 886 soldiers.

From Ramsgate, the first convoy of 'little ships' sailed at 22.00 on 29 May. By the next day they were streaming across the Channel in seemingly unending lines, many of them carrying food and water for the waiting troops. On the bridge of the destroyer HMS *Malcolm*, heading back laden with soldiers from Dunkirk, the sight of the 'little ships' reminded the First Lieutenant of the St Crispin's Day speech in Shakespeare's *Henry V*, delivered by the king on the eve of the battle of Agincourt:

'And Gentlemen in England now abed
Shall think themselves accurs'd they were
    not here.'

'BEF Evacuated' (2 June)

By this time, nobody had any illusions as to the dangers, but fortunately throughout the evacuation the seas remained abnormally calm. At first a huge pall of smoke hid Dunkirk harbour, giving a measure of protection, but when a breeze blew it clear on the afternoon of 29 May, over 400 German aircraft attacked. Despite their best efforts, the Royal Air Force could not entirely deflect such massed attacks, and in the crowded conditions at the end of the mole, the bombers could hardly miss. The destroyer *Jaguar* was damaged; HMS *Grenade* was hit and later blew up. The paddle-minesweeper *Waverley* was bombed on the way home with the loss of over 400 troops. The passenger ships *Lorina* and *Normannia* were bombed and sunk.

Ships faced other hazards. The French destroyer *Bourrasque*, with 800 on board, hit a mine on 30 May. The previous night, the destroyer HMS *Wakeful*, laden with over 600 troops, was torpedoed off the Kwinte buoy and sank in 15 seconds. HMS *Grafton*, with 800 troops on board, was torpedoed as she stopped to rescue the few survivors. In the wake of this tragedy, Ramsay had to signal: 'Vessels carrying troops, not to stop to pick up survivors from ships sunk but are to inform other nearby ships.' Sunken ships also made navigation dangerous. The elderly minesweeper *Brighton Belle* sank after colliding with a hidden wreck; her 800 troops were rescued by the *Medway Queen*.

Left: French soldiers and sailors from the destroyer Bourrasque, *which was hit by a mine on 30 May, awaiting rescue*

Below: A destroyer packed with rescued troops arriving at Dover harbour on 31 May 1940. At the height of the evacuation the vessels lay alongside the quay three or four deep

Right: Charles Cundall's
The Withdrawal from
Dunkirk, June 1940, *which
was commissioned soon
after the event*

Facing page, top to bottom:
*British troops disembarking
at Dover; a wounded soldier
being given a drink on the
quayside; tea being served to
evacuated troops on a train
after arrival at a London
station on 31 May 1940*

On 29 May Ramsay told his wife: 'Everyone is stretched to the limit, doing magnificently … Officers and men cannot continue at this pace, but all are doing their best.' That day so many destroyers were sunk or damaged that the Admiralty reluctantly withdrew the eight newest and largest, in the knowledge that they would be vital in future battles. But destroyers and passenger ships were even more crucial in this battle, for only they had the capacity to carry large numbers of troops. In desperation, on 30 May Ramsay telephoned the First Sea Lord, and six of the eight destroyers were returned to him.

In Dunkirk, troops waited, sheltering in cellars and houses; on the beaches they sought protection in the sand dunes. Makeshift jetties were built using army lorries. Everywhere, troops queued, long lines snaking into the water. On 30 May, heavy cloud prevented air attacks, but 1 June was fine and clear. In the early morning the warships *Havant, Keith* and *Skipjack* were sunk. By evening 31 ships had been destroyed and 11 were seriously damaged. Abandoned and blazing vessels lay all along the beaches. It was clear that from then on the evacuation would have to be restricted to the hours of darkness. That evening Ramsay sent eight destroyers and seven passenger ships to the east mole; numerous smaller vessels headed for the beaches. Navigation lights were banned, adding to the hazards. Despite the disasters of the day,

nearly 65,000 troops were picked up, bringing the tally of those saved to 287,000.

The following day, Ramsay attempted to rescue the stretcher-case wounded in broad daylight. The hospital ships *Worthing* and *Paris*, clearly marked with red crosses like their sister ship, the *Dinard*, sailed unescorted from Dover. Subjected to ferocious air attacks and sustaining considerable damage, they were forced to abandon their mission.

That evening, Ramsay despatched an even larger force, with 13 passenger ships, 14 minesweepers and 11 destroyers at its centre. At 23.30 Captain Tennant sent the historic signal from Dunkirk: 'BEF evacuated.'

Above: An evacuated soldier,
wearing a French overcoat,
changes his socks and boots
on the quayside at Dover,
31 May 1940. Behind him
are piles of stretchers to take
the wounded off the ships
Below: Debris left behind on
the beach at Dunkirk

Final Evacuations (3 June)

By now, German forces were nearly at the outskirts of the town. Only one more evacuation was possible. On the night of 3 June a final effort was made using British, French, Belgian and Dutch ships to rescue as many of the French rearguard as possible. Over 26,000 were saved. The final tally of those rescued and landed in England had exceeded the most optimistic forecasts made at the start, nine days earlier. The heart of the operation had depended on the large ships – the Navy's destroyers and minesweepers embarked nearly 143,000 men and the larger merchant ships nearly 88,000 – but the smaller trawlers and drifters had brought back just under 18,000 men, while the Dutch 'skoots' had saved more than 22,500.

The last Royal Navy ship to enter Dunkirk harbour on 3 June was a small motor torpedo boat. Her captain recorded:

'The night was very dark and full of rushing shapes, all of which appeared to be coming directly at us. They were the last of the rescue ships completing their final task. The flames over the city did not seem so fierce as the night before, but the pall of smoke, which none who saw it will ever forget, still streamed westward from the dying town, and the ring of gun flashes had closed in in an ever narrowing circle. … The whole scene was filled with a sense of finality and death; the curtain was ringing down on a great tragedy.'

A week before, it might have been total tragedy, with most of the British Army lost. But on 4 June Prime Minister Winston Churchill was able to say to a packed House of Commons: 'When a week ago I asked the House to fix this afternoon for a statement, I feared it would be my hard lot to announce from this box the greatest military disaster in our long history.' Instead, he was able to tell them of the extraordinary evacuation, the 'miracle of Dunkirk' in which about 338,000 troops were brought back – the whole of the BEF at Dunkirk and 139,000 French soldiers. But Churchill warned his listeners: 'We must be very careful not to assign to this deliverance the attributes of a victory. Wars are not won by evacuations.'

The evacuation had come at a high price. Of the 693 British ships that had taken part, 188 of the smaller craft had been sunk, as well as eight passenger ships, a hospital ship, trawlers, minesweepers, a sloop and six destroyers. Many had been seriously damaged – only 13 of more than 40 destroyers remained fit for immediate service. On 4 June, in a message to all participants, Ramsay praised their 'fine seamanship combined with indomitable courage and endurance and the very effective co-operation and support afforded us by the Royal Air Force'. But had it not also been for his organizing genius, leadership and drive in his command centre underneath Dover Castle, the evacuation might never have achieved its extraordinary results. Certainly a press correspondent, David Divine, who himself manned one of the 'little ships', had no doubts, later writing:

'It is given to few men to command a miracle. It was so given to Bertram Home Ramsay, and the frail iron balcony that juts from the embrasure of the old casemate in the Dover cliff was the quarter deck from which he commanded one of the great campaigns in the sea story of Britain.'

Daily Express

No. 12,487   Friday, May 31, 1940   One Penny

Through an inferno of bombs and shells the B.E.F. is crossing the Channel from Dunkirk—in history's strangest armada

TENS OF THOUSANDS SAFELY HOME ALREADY

Many more coming by day and night

SHIPS OF ALL SIZES DARE THE GERMAN GUNS

UNDER THE GUNS OF THE BRITISH FLEET, UNDER THE WINGS OF THE ROYAL AIR FORCE, A LARGE PROPORTION OF THE B.E.F. WHO FOR THREE DAYS HAD BEEN FIGHTING THEIR WAY BACK TO THE FLANDERS COAST, HAVE NOW BEEN BROUGHT SAFELY TO ENGLAND FROM DUNKIRK.

First to return were the wounded. An armada of ships—all sizes, all shapes—were used for crossing the Channel. The weather which helped Hitler's tanks to advance has since helped the British evacuation.

Cost to the Navy of carrying out, in an inferno of bombs and shells, one of the most magnificent operations in history has been three destroyers, some auxiliary craft, and a small steamer.

Cost to the enemy of the Fleet's intervention outside Dunkirk can be counted in the shattering of German advanced forces by naval guns and the survival of tens of thousands of British soldiers whom the Germans had hoped to capture or destroy.

THE NAVY CARRIES ON

THREE DESTROYERS LOST
As Navy helps B.E.F.

THE Admiralty issued this communiqué last night:—
The Royal Navy has been and is giving all possible

Tired, dirty, hungry they came back —unbeatable
By HILDE MARCHANT

THE Army is coming back from Belgium. It is a dirty, tired, hungry army. An army that has been shelled and bombed from three sides, and had

Signposts to be removed

SIR JOHN REITH, Minister of Transport, announced last night that "highways authorities . . . are given powers to remove signposts and direction indications which would be of value to the enemy in case of invasion. The work was put in hand on Wednesday."

Gracie goes to America

WITH a red, white and blue rosette in her travelling coat, Gracie Fields and her husband Monty Banks left for America last night from a north-west port.

They announced on Tuesday that they were going. Then a few hours afterwards Monty Banks said: "I am not going now." Only their closest friends knew they had changed their minds again.

Gracie refused to be photographed.

STOP PRESS

FRENCH SAVE PLANES FOR COUNTER ATTACK
—Russian Report.

Russian military expert declared from Moscow last night: "The French counter-attack which is now being planned will take place in the Relhel area. For this counter-attack French are keeping back their planes.

"This is very noticeable and only British air force is now heavily engaged in intense air activity in battle in Flanders. Success of British air force have been very considerable in relation to their numbers."

and did not come on deck from her stateroom, although several officials wished to see her.

How the Allies fought back to Dunkirk, aided by warships and planes. British troops held the left flank, French troops the right flank. Last rearguard action (see inset) fought by French under General Prioux on the hills between Cassel and Ypres.

Dunkirk: Myth and Reality

The German victory over the British and French armies and the surrender of France later in June 1940 left Britain weak, isolated and vulnerable and under threat of imminent invasion. The British Army had abandoned or destroyed virtually all its heavy equipment at Dunkirk. Given time, this could be replaced. But by rescuing the bulk of the Army, Operation Dynamo returned to Britain the priceless asset of the majority of her trained and experienced troops. General Brooke, once an instructor at the Imperial Defence College with Ramsay and after Dunkirk commander-in-chief, Home Forces, was to write: 'Had the BEF not returned to this country, it is hard to see how the Army could have recovered from this blow.'

Of almost equal importance was the psychological effect on the nation. The successfully fought evacuation across seas unusually calm for the nine days was commonly referred to as 'the miracle of Dunkirk'. This in turn engendered the phrase 'the Dunkirk spirit', reflecting a nation united and working against seemingly impossible odds to thwart Hitler's ambitions. By the middle of September the Royal Air Force had won the Battle of Britain, while the Royal Navy remained powerful and undefeated. A successful German invasion was by no means a foregone conclusion.

The phrase 'the Dunkirk spirit' reflected a nation united and working against seemingly impossible odds to thwart Hitler's ambitions

*Above: On 1 July 1940,
Hermann Goering (sixth from
right) and senior German
officers look across the Straits
of Dover to a Britain preparing
for a German invasion*

*Below: A Home Guard squad
prepares to deal with an
invader by means of Molotov
cocktails, during training in the
Dover area in March 1941*

DOVER ON THE FRONT LINE
Hellfire Corner

Preparations to counter a German invasion were under way before Operation Dynamo was over, and were to be intensified following the fall of France later that June. At Dover, the castle was once again a frontier fortress, a key stronghold in the circle of defences around the town and harbour. On 1 June the garrison was ordered to be 'in an instant state of readiness to deal with enemy attack'; the men were to 'sleep fully armed in or adjacent to section posts and road blocks'. The overgrown slit trenches on the outer earthworks of the castle date from these desperate months, as do the concrete 'dragon's teeth' tank defences at the northern spur and a small concrete pillbox at the foot of Horseshoe Bastion. This last was one of a series constructed around the defensive perimeter of Dover, some manned by the Home Guard and by early September linked by a belt of barbed wire.

After Dunkirk the acute shortage of military equipment meant the garrison had to improvise, as on 2 June when they were ordered to make

Molotov bombs. Bottles with corks were 'to be obtained by collection and local purchase if necessary', while petrol and matches would be provided by 'military channels'. On 18 June, as invasion fears mounted, the garrison was warned not to be misled by the actions of German parachutists:

'The only weapons available to the parachutist during the jump are a pistol … and several small hand grenades. … If he anticipates resistance … he ho ds a hand grenade in each of his hands which he holds above his head so that he is in a ready position to throw them. This holding of the hands above the head should not be confused with a desire to surrender.'

Together with Fort Burgoyne and Western Heights, the castle was designated as a location 'to be defended to the last' and was provisioned to withstand a six-week siege, a precaution probably last implemented here on this scale before the great siege of 1216. It was probably at this time that demolition charges were placed at key points in the castle, to be detcnated if necessary to prevent it from falling into enemy hands. On 18 August bombs falling on the castle and Fort Burgoyne killed 10 and wounded 24 personnel.

In the Straits, British convoys were subjected to ferocious air attacks, which in July forced the Admiralty to restrict merchant ships to night-time sailing. When intelligence was received of German cross-Channel guns the larger warships were briefly withdrawn to Sheerness and Harwich. Overhead, the Battle of Britain was fought from mid-July to mid-September. Although the defeat of the Luftwaffe signalled the end of any invasion during 1940, the threat remained real until 1942.

In the next four years the area acquired its name of 'Hellfire Corner', a target for German bombers and cross-Channel guns at Cap Gris Nez. There was constant skirmishing between German E-boats and the motor torpedo boats and motor gunboats of the Royal Navy. Long-range guns on both shores fired across the Straits, usually at convoys or single merchantmen attempting the dangerous passage. Occasionally there were greater excitements, as on 12 February 1942 when the powerful German battle-cruisers *Scharnhorst* and *Gneisenau* and the cruiser *Prinz*

Left: Civilians sheltering in the town caves at Dover
Below: *Soldiers guarding the beach at Dover behind a barbed wire barricade, in about 1940*

Eugen staged their daring dash through the Straits, flanked by flotillas of destroyers and torpedo boats and with an umbrella of fighters above. The six naval Swordfish planes sent to attack them were all shot down; their leader, Lieutenant-Commander Esmonde, was awarded a posthumous Victoria Cross.

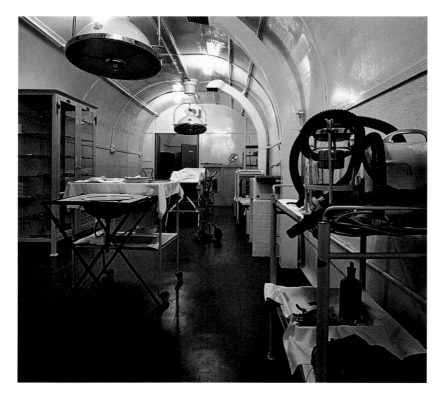

Above: A reconstructed operating theatre in Annexe level, the new complex of tunnels built in 1941–2
Below: Part of Annexe level in use as living quarters, drawn by the war artist Anthony Gross in 1941
Below right: A hospital tunnel in Annexe level in use during the war

The Tunnels after Dunkirk

Within the secure tunnels beneath the castle, all enemy activity was monitored and action authorized by the commanders. Information was relayed to the RAF and to the Admiralty and War Office in London. It arrived from coastal observers, pilots and warships and from the new radar chain, some of whose lattice masts remain prominent features on the cliff-top east of the castle. By 1943 the Navy had acquired its own radar set to monitor shipping; the hexagonal brick base stands on the cliff edge near the end of the eastern ramparts. The Navy also employed Wrens (members of the Women's Royal Naval Service) who were fluent in German next to the cipher room in Admiralty Casemate to monitor German forces' wireless transmissions. As further coastal gun batteries were installed, they were linked to the gun operations room, which by 1941 controlled some 4,500 personnel and batteries from the North Foreland (north of Ramsgate) as far west as Hastings.

In the summer of 1941 proposals were put forward for an underground medical dressing station, where casualties could be attended to in safety before being sent to hospitals away from the bombing and shelling of Dover. The chosen site was higher up within the cliffs above the existing Casemate level. The project was authorized in August and the work was undertaken by 171 Tunnelling Company of the Royal Engineers, and completed early the following January.

The new complex of tunnels, named Annexe, was designed on a grid system, with large communication tunnels and smaller ones at right angles for reception areas, wards, operating theatres, ablutions, kitchen and stores. For speed, the tunnels employed the standard metal linings used in coal mines. The entrance to Annexe was just above Canon's Gate, and its far end was linked to the existing spiral stair down to Casemate level. The tunnels had been completed, but installation of hospital equipment had not been started by the following August, when changes of plan caused the work to be halted.

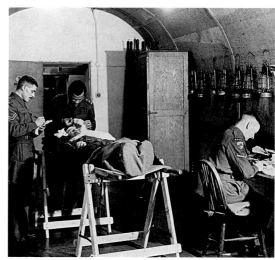

Combined Headquarters

By 1942 military planners had realized that a bombproof combined headquarters for all three services would be needed close to the launching point in Britain for an invasion of German-occupied Europe. These headquarters had to accommodate substantial numbers of people – the Army alone estimated its requirement for staff, working in shifts, at 150 officers and 500 other ranks. Later that year, construction of such a combined headquarters (CHQ) was started near Portsmouth, but as no final decision had yet been taken on the precise destination for what became Operation Overlord, it was decided to build two further CHQs, one at Devonport and one in Kent. After a location at Folkestone had been considered, approval was given in December 1942 for one below Dover Castle, to take advantage of the existing facilities.

Excluding passages, about 30,000 sq. ft (2,800 sq. m) was required. This time, a much larger grid of tunnels compared to the medical dressing station was excavated about 15m below Casemate. At its centre were the operations rooms, with about 9,000 sq. ft (800 sq. m) allocated for communications equipment. During the peak of the operation some 660 men of the 172 Tunnelling Company, Royal Engineers, were employed. The new level, later named Dumpy, was linked to Casemate level by two staircases and was completed in May 1943.

The influx of staff needed for the new CHQ put a severe strain on accommodation. Even the derelict 18th-century barracks in the inner bailey were made habitable, although only their ground and first floors were used to avoid too great a concentration of personnel in case of bombardment, something the military planners feared if an invasion were launched from this area. Secure emergency sleeping accommodation for the headquarters staff was another priority. The fitting out of the new medical dressing station had been halted the previous August to see whether these tunnels could be used as dormitories. The following February a compromise was reached: five wards could be used as dormitories, but the hospital would retain 105 bed spaces.

On Casemate level itself, space was at a premium. The proliferation of extra communications equipment led in 1942 to

Left: Sappers digging a tunnel during the construction of an underground command centre near Seaford, Sussex, in October 1941

Below: A naval office in Admiralty Casemate, one of many rooms created in the tunnels with timber partitions

the digging of a tunnel west of and parallel to the three eastern tunnels. The General Post Office, which was in charge of all land communications, needed the space for the dozens of batteries and battery-charging equipment used by the telephones and teleprinters. Early in 1943 a communications tunnel was excavated from the

Right: The reconstructed
coastal artillery operations
room today
Below: A wartime
photograph of the coastal
artillery operations room

rear communications tunnel. The new tunnel gave direct access to the coastal artillery operations room in the central of the three eastern tunnels, thus bypassing the northern half of the casemate, which was filled with Post Office equipment. This was completed soon after Royal Artillery personnel had undertaken what were described

as 'amateur and unauthorised excavations', using material scrounged from naval sources, to create a small combined Royal Artillery and Royal Naval operations room between the easternmost casemate – Admiralty Casemate – and the central tunnel, which housed the coastal artillery staff. This might have escaped the notice of headquarters had not the unauthorized work cracked brickwork in the Admiralty tunnel. It was recognized, however, that such a joint operations room was now essential, as the coastal batteries were concentrating on closing the Channel to enemy shipping using radar to find their targets, and needed naval assistance to identify these.

The combined headquarters started operating in the summer of 1943, with the navy, coastal artillery and much of the communications equipment remaining in Casemate level. There were ambitious plans to excavate further tunnels, but these were never realized. For the rest of the war Dover continued to play a vital role, not least at the time of the Normandy invasion in 1944, which was controlled from the Portsmouth CHQ. Dover then had a valuable supporting role in Operation Fortitude, the elaborate and successful deception that convinced the Germans

SECTION LOOKING EAST

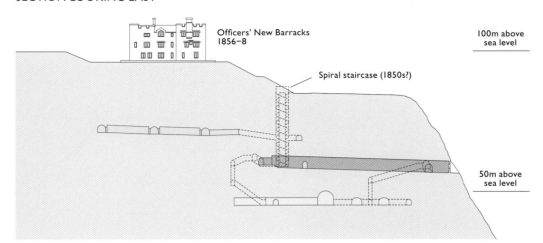

Officers' New Barracks 1856–8

Spiral staircase (1850s?)

100m above sea level

50m above sea level

Left: Cross-section and plan of the tunnels, showing the complex network of tunnels on three levels developed during and after the Second World War from the original Georgian tunnels

PLAN

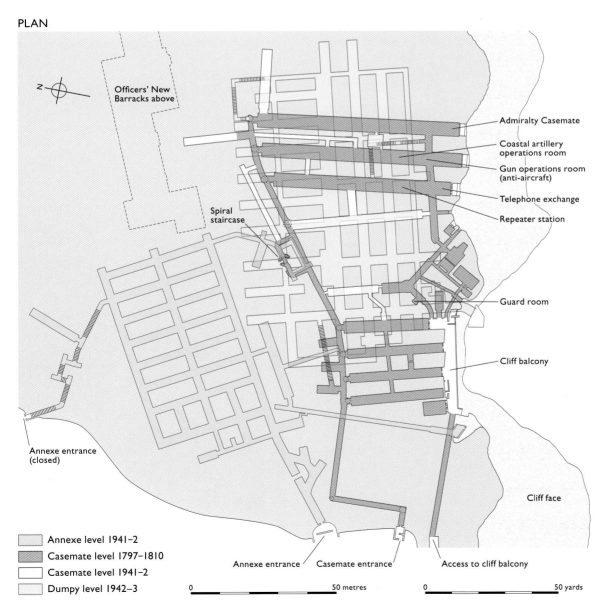

Officers' New Barracks above

Spiral staircase

Admiralty Casemate

Coastal artillery operations room

Gun operations room (anti-aircraft)

Telephone exchange

Repeater station

Guard room

Cliff balcony

Cliff face

Annexe entrance (closed)

Annexe entrance

Casemate entrance

Access to cliff balcony

Annexe level 1941–2

Casemate level 1797–1810

Casemate level 1941–2

Dumpy level 1942–3

0   50 metres

0   50 yards

Above: The reconstructed repeater station. Such repeater stations were needed at approximately 10 mile intervals to amplify telephone messages passing along land lines

existence. The atmosphere was frequently chilly and damp, while the lack of daylight and the constant background roar of the forced ventilation added to feelings of tiredness. There was little time, however, for considerations of personal discomfort, especially in the months after Dunkirk. As the number of staff increased, the layout in the old tunnels was frequently modified to reconfigure office spaces. The new tunnels were better planned, but their corrugated metal walls and utilitarian office furniture ensured a spartan atmosphere. Many service and civilian personnel who worked here recalled the importance of a respect for security.

Superficially, the Second World War made little impact on the appearance of the rest of the castle, for the heart of its defence effort lay hidden beneath it. Appropriately the most immediately visible relics reflect the new dimension of warfare: the sites of the four light anti-aircraft guns on the eastern ramparts, the base of the naval radar nearby, and the massive reinforced concrete roof added in 1941 to protect the Fire Command Post and Port War Signal Station from bombs. Fittingly, in November 2000 a statue of Vice-Admiral Sir Bertram Ramsay was unveiled nearby.

at a critical time that the real invasion would be in the Pas de Calais.

All those who worked in these tunnels, especially in the early years when there were only minimal comforts and basic facilities, recall long hours, the uneven chalk passages in Casemate level, and the strain and weariness of underground

Working in Wartime Dover Castle

Mary Horsfall (*right*), a young WRNS officer posted to Ramsay's staff early in 1942, recalls the impact of the castle on those serving there: 'Suddenly here you are – confronted with Dover Castle, which is so tremendously strong, wonderfully British, wonderfully English. It's been there, it's stuck it out all that time and nothing is ever going to change that and I think that made a profound impression on us ... it looked all chunky and

tremendous, it held everything together. I don't think we talked about it, but I think we all felt it.'

When Churchill visited, he asked Mary if she was frightened when German guns were shelling Dover: 'I burst out laughing and I said "Good Gracious, No Sir", laughing, and I got into terrible trouble for having laughed at the Prime Minister. But it came from the heart, it had never entered our heads, it was part of the job. There was no fear, no, nothing attached to it at all.'

POST-WAR DOVER AND THE COLD WAR

In 1945 the castle slowly resumed its former peacetime life as a garrison headquarters. But its magnificent setting and distinguished military history did not compensate for the disadvantages of obsolete barracks, the absence of space for new ones, and the lack of access for all except the smallest military vehicles. In 1958 the Army vacated the castle with the exception of Constable's Gate. In 1963 the whole castle came into the care of the Ministry of Works, predecessor of English Heritage, which had been looking after parts of it since 1904.

The combined headquarters closed in 1945, but the hospital continued to serve the garrison until its departure. This was the time of the Cold War, a period of growing international tension and fear of the Soviet Union's intentions. In 1962 the Cuban Missile Crisis led many to fear that the three-minute warning of nuclear attack was about to become a ghastly reality.

The British government, concerned that a nuclear war would wipe out London and the machinery of government, had already started constructing 12 Regional Seats of Government. These were located in relatively secure accommodation and when in use would be in the charge of a senior minister designated as a regional commissioner. Aided by a small team of civilian and military advisers, they would have virtually unfettered powers over any surviving population. Their instructions were not encouraging. After fire-fighting, rescue and first-aid for victims amid the radioactive carnage of a post-nuclear Britain, their tasks were to ensure a degree of law and order, look after survivors, make best use of remaining resources and maintain some semblance of administration. It was assumed that each region would have to act virtually independently of any other.

Amid conditions of great secrecy, the Dover tunnels were selected as one of the Regional Seats. They required considerable modernization for this task. The Home Office installed new communications equipment, modern air-filtration plant and improved generators. The old spiral staircase had its top capped with concrete as a precaution against nuclear contamination and a lift was installed. Space was allocated for substantial

reserves of fuel, water and food. The former medical dressing station was designated as sleeping quarters and needed comparatively little work, save for the installation of two-tier bunk beds and an airlock at its entrance.

On Casemate level, all the cliff entrances were sealed against radioactive contamination and the four western tunnels were allocated as dining areas. Upper floors were inserted, along with catering facilities, rest rooms and more dormitories. These remain much as they were when completed in the early 1960s. The three eastern tunnels – once Ramsay's headquarters, the command centre for coastal artillery, the anti-aircraft operations room and the main telephone exchange – were not used, and were stripped of their contents, although the Admiralty retained an interest here into the early 1980s. The operational heart of the Regional Seat of Government was in the lowest level of tunnels, Dumpy, where the larger spaces were more readily adaptable. Further modernizations were undertaken and regular weekend exercises were held into the early 1980s, when the Home Office reorganized the system and abandoned the Dover tunnels, after removing virtually all their equipment.

Above: Dover Castle shown on a 1974 Soviet army map. The Russians prepared maps of 103 British towns and cities for use during an invasion

Below: A contamination monitor made in the 1960s by Plessey Electronics to measure radioactivity after a nuclear attack

Right: The castle today, seen from the sea, showing the cliff entrance to Casemate level (centre); the window of Ramsay's cabin, at the end of Admiralty Casemate, is visible on the far right
Below: The view from the Casemate balcony

THE TUNNELS TODAY

The castle and tunnels provide a vivid illustration of changing warfare over the past two centuries. Massive ramparts, moats, gun positions and barracks reflect the medieval castle's adaptation as an artillery fortress guarding the overland approach to Dover. Below ground, the Georgian tunnels demonstrate the ingenuity of military engineers in creating accommodation for the wartime garrison. These and the later additions to the tunnels are witness to the increasingly destructive power of weapons and the need in a front-line location for a secure headquarters and military hospital.

The tunnels' evolving use is apparent in their architecture and equipment. Much of the equipment on display now is original; some was once used here, while other pieces are accurate replicas made after careful research. The brick-vaulted tunnels, the narrower linking tunnels with their great ventilation shafts and the brick-domed well-head demonstrate the sophistication and scale of these underground barracks. The three eastern tunnels and their

wartime extensions are displayed to show aspects of these tunnels as they appeared during the Second World War, and more specifically in the summer of 1941 and later. The four western tunnels, including the kitchen and upper floors, reflect their final use as part of the Regional Seat of Government.

The medical dressing station on Annexe level, its utilitarian metal linings in sharp contrast to the brickwork in the tunnels below, is displayed partly as a wartime hospital and partly as wartime dormitory accommodation as reused by the Regional Seat of Government. The bunk beds were probably installed here in the 1960s; the medical equipment on display largely dates from the 1940s and is now arranged as shown in photographs taken in 1945.

The cliff tunnels beneath Dover Castle remain a unique complex with an unparalleled history. Designed as secure barracks during the Napoleonic Wars, they were to play their greatest role in the early summer of 1940. Thankfully, in their final phase, they were never put to the test.

ACKNOWLEDGEMENTS

English Heritage and the author would particularly like to thank the following for their assistance in the preparation of this guide: Gill Arnott, Mary Horsfall, Jon Iveson, Paul Pattison, Vic Viner and Rowena Willard-Wright. The extract from Daphne Baker's memoir is reproduced by courtesy of Candy Balfour and Luli Harvey.

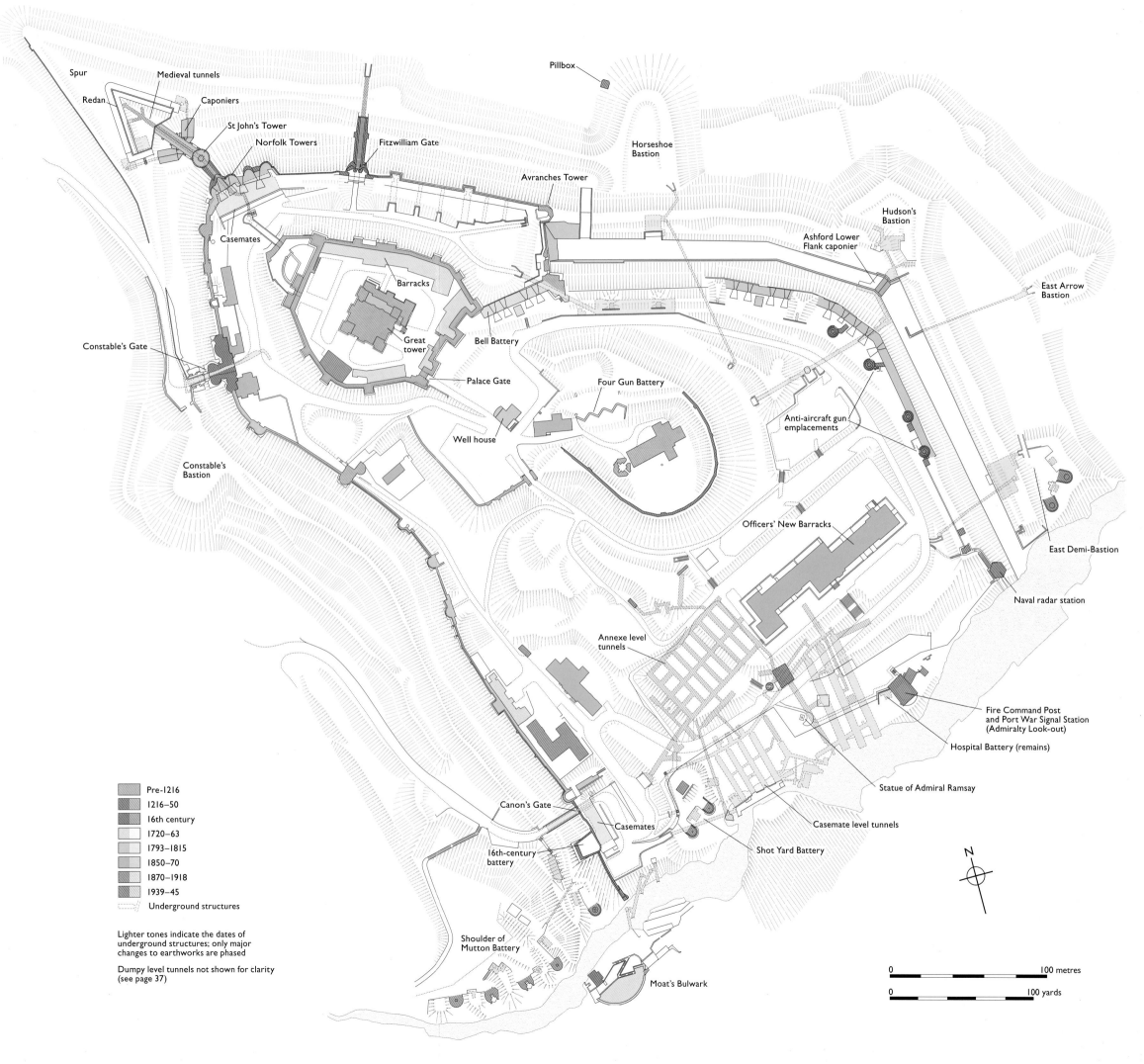

Spur
Redan
Medieval tunnels
Caponiers
St John's Tower
Norfolk Towers
Fitzwilliam Gate
Pillbox
Horseshoe Bastion
Avranches Tower
Hudson's Bastion
Ashford Lower Flank caponier
East Arrow Bastion
Casemates
Barracks
Great tower
Bell Battery
Constable's Gate
Palace Gate
Four Gun Battery
Anti-aircraft gun emplacements
Well house
Constable's Bastion
Officers' New Barracks
East Demi-Bastion
Naval radar station
Annexe level tunnels
Fire Command Post and Port War Signal Station (Admiralty Look-out)
Hospital Battery (remains)
Statue of Admiral Ramsay
Casemate level tunnels
Canon's Gate
Casemates
16th-century battery
Shot Yard Battery
Shoulder of Mutton Battery
Moat's Bulwark

Pre-1216
1216–50
16th century
1720–63
1793–1815
1850–70
1870–1918
1939–45
Underground structures

Lighter tones indicate the dates of underground structures; only major changes to earthworks are phased

Dumpy level tunnels not shown for clarity (see page 37)

N

0   100 metres
0   100 yards